ELIXIR

THE FUTURE OF CONCURRENT PROGRAMMING

OLIVER LUCAS JR

PREFACE

Elixir: A Functional Approach to Scalable and Reliable Systems

In an era of ever-increasing complexity and demand for real-time, scalable applications, Elixir emerges as a powerful and elegant solution. This book is your guide to mastering Elixir, a functional programming language designed to build robust and efficient systems.

Whether you're a seasoned developer or just starting your journey into the world of programming, Elixir offers a unique and rewarding experience. Its concise syntax, strong focus on concurrency, and built-in fault tolerance make it an ideal choice for a wide range of applications.

Throughout this book, you'll explore:

Core Concepts: Dive into the fundamentals of functional programming, including immutability, pattern matching, and recursion.

The Elixir Ecosystem: Discover the rich ecosystem of libraries and frameworks, such as Phoenix, Ecto, and Nerves.

Concurrency and Parallelism: Harness the power of the Erlang VM to build highly concurrent and scalable applications.

Real-Time Applications: Learn how to build real-time web applications with Phoenix LiveView.

Fault Tolerance and Error Handling: Master techniques for building resilient systems.

Advanced Topics: Explore advanced concepts like metaprogramming, OTP behaviors, and distributed systems.

This book is not just a technical reference; it's an invitation to a new way of thinking about software development. By the end of this journey, you'll be equipped to create exceptional Elixir applications that are both powerful and elegant.

Let's embark on this exciting adventure together.

TABLET OF CONTENTS

Chapter 5

Chapter 6

Chapter 7

Chapter 8

Chapter 9

Chapter 10

Chapter 1

Introduction to Elixir

1.1 What is Elixir?

Elixir is a dynamic, functional programming language designed for building scalable and maintainable applications. It runs on the Erlang Virtual Machine (BEAM), known for its ability to create low-latency, distributed, and fault-tolerant systems.

Key features of Elixir:

Functional programming: Elixir embraces functional programming principles like immutability, pure functions, and pattern matching, leading to cleaner, more predictable, and easier-to-test code.

Concurrency and parallelism: Elixir leverages the power of the Actor model, allowing you to build highly concurrent and parallel applications that can handle a large number of concurrent users and tasks efficiently.

Fault tolerance: Elixir's built-in mechanisms for error handling and supervision trees make it possible to create systems that can recover from failures gracefully.

Hot code reloading: You can modify your code and see the changes reflected in your running application without restarting it, significantly speeding up development cycles.

Extensibility: Elixir's metaprogramming capabilities allow you to extend the language itself, creating domain-specific languages (DSLs) tailored to your specific needs.

Common use cases for Elixir:

Web development: Elixir's Phoenix framework provides a robust and efficient way to build scalable web applications.

Real-time applications: Elixir's ability to handle a large number of concurrent connections makes it ideal for building real-time applications like chat apps, multiplayer games, and IoT systems.

Embedded systems: Elixir can be used to create embedded systems that require high performance and reliability.

Data processing pipelines: Elixir's ability to handle large volumes of data and process it in parallel makes it suitable for building data pipelines and data processing systems.

If you're looking for a language that can help you build reliable, scalable, and maintainable applications, Elixir is definitely worth considering.

1.2 Why Elixir?

Why Elixir?

Elixir offers a compelling blend of features that make it an excellent choice for building robust, scalable, and maintainable applications. Here are some key reasons why you might consider using Elixir:

1. Concurrency and Fault Tolerance:

Built on the BEAM: Elixir leverages the powerful Erlang VM (BEAM), renowned for its ability to handle massive concurrency and distribute workloads across multiple cores and machines.

Actor Model: Elixir's actor model simplifies concurrent programming, enabling you to write highly scalable applications without the complexity of traditional threading.

Fault Tolerance: The BEAM's supervision trees ensure that your application can recover gracefully from errors and failures, making it highly resilient.

2. Functional Programming Paradigm:

Immutability: Elixir's emphasis on immutability reduces side effects and makes code more predictable and easier to reason about.

Pure Functions: By writing pure functions, you can isolate logic, test it independently, and compose complex systems from simpler building blocks.

Pattern Matching: Elixir's powerful pattern matching allows you to concisely express complex data transformations and control flow.

3. Productivity and Developer Experience:

Expressive Syntax: Elixir's syntax is clean, concise, and inspired by Ruby, making it easy to learn and write.

Hot Code Reloading: You can make changes to your code and see the effects immediately, without restarting your application.

Strong Community and Ecosystem: Elixir boasts a vibrant community and a growing ecosystem of libraries and frameworks, such as Phoenix, for web development and Nerves for embedded systems.

4. Scalability and Performance:

Distributed Systems: Elixir's built-in support for distributed systems enables you to scale your applications horizontally across multiple nodes.

High Performance: The BEAM's efficient memory management and optimized bytecode execution ensure that Elixir applications can handle high loads and deliver low latency.

In summary, Elixir is a powerful language that empowers developers to build reliable, scalable, and maintainable applications with ease. Its unique combination of features, coupled with its strong community and ecosystem, makes it an excellent choice for a wide range of projects.

1.3 Setting Up Your Elixir Development Environment

Prerequisites:

A computer: A Mac, Windows, or Linux machine will work.

Basic terminal or command prompt knowledge.

Installation:

1. Install Elixir:

Using a package manager:

macOS: Use Homebrew:

Bash

brew install elixir

Linux: Use your distribution's package manager (e.g., apt, yum, dnf):
Bash
# Ubuntu/Debian:
sudo apt install elixir

# Fedora/CentOS:
sudo dnf install elixir

Manual installation: Download the latest Elixir installer from the official website and follow the instructions.

2. Install a Package Manager (Optional but Highly Recommended):

Elixir's package manager, `mix`: Comes bundled with Elixir. You'll use it to manage dependencies, compile projects, and run tests.

Verifying Installation:

Open your terminal or command prompt.

Type `elixir -v` and press Enter. You should see the Elixir version.

Type `iex` and press Enter. You'll enter the interactive Elixir shell.

Creating a New Elixir Project:

Open your terminal.

Navigate to your desired project directory.

Create a new project:

Bash

mix new my_project

1. Replace `my_project` with your desired project name.

Running Your First Elixir Project:

1. **Navigate to your project directory:**
2. Bash

cd my_project

3.
4.
5. **Start the IEx shell:**
6. Bash

iex -S mix

7.
8.
9. **Try a simple expression:**
10. Elixir

iex> 2 + 2

11.
12.

A Basic Elixir Project Structure:

An Elixir project typically has the following structure:

my_project/
├── mix.exs
├── lib/

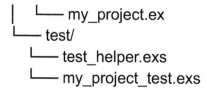

```
|     └── my_project.ex
└── test/
    └── test_helper.exs
    └── my_project_test.exs
```

mix.exs: Defines project metadata and dependencies.
lib/my_project.ex: Contains your project's modules and functions
test/test_helper.exs: Contains configuration for tests.
test/my_project_test.exs: Contains your project's test cases.

Additional Tips:

Use a good code editor or IDE: Visual Studio Code, Emacs, Vim, and IntelliJ IDEA are popular choices.

Explore Elixir's documentation: The official Elixir documentation is a great resource.

Join the Elixir community: There are many online forums and communities where you can ask questions and learn from others.

Practice regularly: The best way to learn Elixir is to practice.

By following these steps, you'll be well on your way to becoming an Elixir developer.

Chapter 2

Functional Programming with Elixir

2.1 Core Concepts of Functional Programming

Functional programming is a programming paradigm that treats computation as the evaluation of mathematical functions and avoids changing state and mutable data.[1] Here are some of its core concepts:

1. Pure Functions:

Input-Output Mapping: A pure function always produces the same output for a given input.

No Side Effects: It doesn't modify any external state or have any observable effect beyond its return value.

Benefits: Easier to test, reason about, and compose with other functions.

2. Immutability:

Unchanging Data: Data in functional programming is generally immutable, meaning it cannot be changed after it's created.

Benefits: Reduces side effects, simplifies reasoning about code, and makes it easier to write concurrent and parallel programs.

3. Higher-Order Functions:

Functions as Arguments and Return Values: Functions can be passed as arguments to other functions or returned as results.

Common Examples: Map, filter, reduce, and compose.

Benefits: Allows for more expressive and concise code.

4. Recursion:

Recursive Functions: Functions that call themselves directly or indirectly.

Base Case and Recursive Case: A recursive function must have a base case to stop the recursion and a recursive case to make progress towards the base case.

Benefits: Can be used to solve problems elegantly, especially those that can be broken down into smaller, self-similar subproblems.

5. First-Class Functions:

Functions as Data: Functions can be treated as data, assigned to variables, passed as arguments, and returned from other functions.

Benefits: Enables flexible and expressive programming styles.

6. Lazy Evaluation:

Delayed Computation: Expressions are only evaluated when their results are needed.

Benefits: Can improve performance, especially in cases where not all parts of a computation are necessary.

By understanding and applying these concepts, you can write more concise, reliable, and maintainable code. Functional programming languages like Elixir, Haskell, and Clojure are designed to promote these principles and provide powerful tools for building complex applications.

2.2 Immutability and Pure Functions

These two concepts are fundamental to functional programming, and they work hand-in-hand to create more predictable, maintainable, and testable code.

Immutability

Definition: Immutability means that once a piece of data is created, its value cannot be changed. Any modification to the data results in a new, distinct piece of data.

Benefits:

Predictability: Immutable data structures make code easier to reason about. If a value doesn't change, you can be sure that it will always have the same value.

Concurrency Safety: Immutable data structures are inherently thread-safe, as multiple threads can access and modify them without worrying about race conditions or data corruption.

Testing: Immutable data structures are easier to test, as you can create test cases with known inputs and outputs without worrying about side effects.

Pure Functions

Definition: A pure function is a function that:

Always returns the same output for the same input.

Has no side effects. That is, it doesn't modify any external state or produce output other than its return value.

Benefits:

Testability: Pure functions are easy to test, as you can simply provide input values and assert the expected output.

Composability: Pure functions can be combined and composed in various ways to create more complex functions.

Referential Transparency: A pure function can be replaced with its return value without affecting the program's behavior.

Why Immutability and Pure Functions Go Hand-in-Hand

Predictable Behavior: By using immutable data structures and pure functions, you can create code that is more predictable and less prone to bugs.

Easier Debugging: If a bug occurs, you can trace the flow of data through your program more easily, as there are no hidden side effects or mutable state to consider.

Parallelism and Concurrency: Immutable data structures and pure functions are well-suited for parallel and concurrent programming, as they can be executed independently without worrying about race conditions or data corruption.

Example:

Consider a simple function to increment a number:

Imperative (mutable):

```
JavaScript
function increment(x) {
  x = x + 1;
  return x;
}
```

Functional (immutable):

```
JavaScript
function increment(x) {
  return x + 1;
}
```

The functional approach is more pure because it doesn't modify the input x but returns a new value. This makes it easier to reason about and test.

By embracing immutability and pure functions, you can write more elegant, reliable, and maintainable code.

2.3 Pattern Matching and Recursion

These two concepts are closely related and are powerful tools in functional programming.

Pattern Matching

Pattern matching is a technique for extracting information from data structures by comparing them to patterns. It's often used to:

Destructure data: Break down complex data structures into simpler components.

Control flow: Make decisions based on the structure of data.

Define recursive functions: Provide elegant solutions to recursive problems.

Example in Elixir:

```
Elixir
defmodule Math do
```

```
  def factorial(0), do: 1
  def factorial(n), do: n * factorial(n - 1)
end
```

In this example, the `factorial/1` function uses pattern matching to define two cases:

Base case: When n is 0, the function returns 1.

Recursive case: When n is greater than 0, the function recursively calls itself with n - 1 and multiplies the result by n.

Recursion

Recursion is a technique where a function calls itself directly or indirectly. It's often used to solve problems that can be broken down[1] into smaller, self-similar subproblems.

Key components of recursion:

Base case: The simplest case that can be solved directly, without recursion.

Recursive case: The case that breaks down the problem into a smaller subproblem and calls the function recursively to solve it.

Example in Elixir:

```
Elixir
defmodule List do
  def sum([]), do: 0
  def sum([head | tail]), do: head + sum(tail)
end
```

In this example, the sum/1 function uses recursion to calculate the sum of a list of numbers:

Base case: If the list is empty, the sum is 0.

Recursive case: If the list is not empty, the function adds the head of the list to the sum of the tail of the list.

By combining pattern matching and recursion, you can write elegant and concise solutions to a wide range of problems in functional programming.

Chapter 3

The Elixir Ecosystem

3.1 The Elixir Toolchain

The Elixir toolchain is a collection of tools and libraries that work together to provide a seamless development experience. Here are some of the key components:

1. Elixir:

The core programming language itself.

Provides a functional programming paradigm, a powerful macro system, and a focus on concurrency and fault tolerance.

2. Erlang VM (BEAM):

The virtual machine that executes Elixir code.

Known for its ability to handle high concurrency, fault tolerance, and distributed systems.

3. Mix:

Elixir's build tool and package manager.

Used to create new projects, manage dependencies, compile code, run tests, and deploy applications.

4. IEx:

Elixir's interactive shell.

Allows you to experiment with Elixir code, test functions, and debug applications.

5. Ecto:

A powerful database abstraction layer for Elixir.

Supports various databases (PostgreSQL, MySQL, SQLite, etc.) and provides features like migrations, queries, and associations.

6. Phoenix:

A high-performance web framework built on top of Elixir.

Offers features like routing, controllers, views, channels, and a robust development experience.

7. Plug:

A specification and set of tools for building HTTP applications in Elixir.

Provides a modular approach to building web applications, allowing you to compose different components (connectors, routers, middleware) to create complex applications.

8. Elixir Ecosystem:

A growing ecosystem of libraries and tools for various tasks, including:

Data processing: Nx, Absinthe

Machine learning: Axon

Real-time applications: Phoenix LiveView

Testing: ExUnit, PropEr

Deployment: Distillery, Mix Releases

By understanding and effectively using these tools, you can build robust, scalable, and maintainable Elixir applications.

3.2 Popular Elixir Libraries and Frameworks

Here are some of the most popular Elixir libraries and frameworks:

Web Development:

Phoenix: A powerful and productive web framework that emphasizes simplicity, speed, and robustness. It's great for building real-time web applications.

Plug: A specification and set of tools for building HTTP applications in Elixir. It provides a modular approach to building web applications.

Database Access:

Ecto: A flexible and powerful database abstraction layer for Elixir. It supports various databases like PostgreSQL, MySQL, SQLite, and more.

Concurrency and Distribution:

OTP (Open Telecom Platform): A suite of behaviors and design patterns for building distributed, fault-tolerant systems. It's the foundation of Elixir's concurrency model.

GenServer: A fundamental building block for creating concurrent, stateful processes in Elixir.

Supervisor: A process that monitors and restarts child processes, ensuring system reliability.

Testing and Debugging:

ExUnit: Elixir's built-in testing framework, providing tools for writing and running tests.

Credo: A static analysis tool for improving Elixir code quality.

Data Processing and Pipelines:

Broadway: A library for building robust, fault-tolerant data processing pipelines.

Other Notable Libraries:

Nerves: A framework for building embedded devices with Elixir.

Absinthe: A GraphQL server implementation for Elixir.

Poison: A library for parsing and generating JSON.

ExMachina: A library for generating test data.

This is just a small sample of the many great libraries and frameworks available in the Elixir ecosystem. The Elixir community is constantly growing and evolving, and new tools are being released all the time.

3.3 Building a Simple Elixir Application

Let's create a basic Elixir application that calculates factorials.

1. Create a New Project:

Bash
```
mix new factorial_app
cd factorial_app
```

2. Define the Factorial Function:

Open the `lib/factorial_app.ex` file and add the following:

Elixir
```
defmodule FactorialApp do
  def factorial(0), do: 1
  def factorial(n), do: n * factorial(n - 1)
end
```

This defines a module `FactorialApp` with a recursive `factorial/1` function.

3. Test the Function:

Open the `test/factorial_app_test.exs` file and add the following:

Elixir
```
defmodule FactorialAppTest do
  use ExUnit.Case
  import FactorialApp

  test "calculates factorial of 0" do
    assert factorial(0) == 1
  end

  test "calculates factorial of 5" do
    assert factorial(5) == 120
  end
end
```

4. Run the Tests:

In your terminal, run:

Bash
mix test

5. Run the Application Interactively:

In your terminal, run:

Bash
iex -S mix

This will start the IEx shell. You can then call the `factorial` function:

Elixir
iex> FactorialApp.factorial(5)
120

Explanation:

Module Definition: We define a module `FactorialApp` to encapsulate our functionality.

Function Definition: The `factorial/1` function is defined recursively. The base case is when n is 0, and the recursive case calculates the factorial of `n-1` and multiplies it by n.

Testing: We use the `ExUnit` testing framework to write unit tests for our `factorial` function.

Interactive Shell: The `iex` shell allows us to interact with our Elixir code directly.

Additional Considerations:

Error Handling: Consider adding error handling for invalid input (e.g., negative numbers).

Performance Optimization: For larger factorials, you might explore tail recursion or memoization techniques.

Deployment: Elixir offers various deployment options, including using a process manager like `Supervisor` or deploying to a cloud platform like Heroku.

By following these steps and exploring the Elixir ecosystem, you can build more complex and sophisticated applications.

Chapter 4

Understanding the BEAM

4.1 The Erlang Virtual Machine (BEAM)

The Erlang Virtual Machine (BEAM) is a powerful virtual machine that powers both Erlang and Elixir. It's renowned for its ability to handle high concurrency, fault tolerance, and distributed systems with ease.

Key Features of the BEAM:

Lightweight Processes: The BEAM excels at managing a massive number of lightweight processes. These processes are isolated from each other, making them highly fault-tolerant. If one process crashes, it won't affect others.

Message Passing: Processes communicate with each other by sending and receiving messages. This asynchronous communication model promotes scalability and resilience.

Hot Code Swapping: You can update code in a running application without downtime. This allows for seamless updates and deployments.

Distributed Systems: The BEAM supports distributed systems, enabling you to build applications that span multiple machines.

Fault Tolerance: The BEAM's supervision trees ensure that processes are monitored and restarted if they fail, leading to highly reliable systems.

High Concurrency: The BEAM efficiently handles a large number of concurrent tasks, making it ideal for real-time applications and systems with high throughput.

How the BEAM Works:

Compilation: Erlang and Elixir source code is compiled into bytecode.

Bytecode Execution: The BEAM executes this bytecode.

Process Scheduling: The BEAM schedules processes efficiently, ensuring that they are executed in a fair and timely manner.

Message Passing: Processes communicate by sending and receiving messages.

Error Handling and Recovery: The BEAM's supervision trees monitor and restart processes that fail, ensuring system reliability.

Elixir and the BEAM:

Elixir leverages the power of the BEAM to provide a modern and expressive language for building scalable and fault-tolerant applications. By using Elixir, you can take advantage of the BEAM's capabilities without the complexity of traditional Erlang.

In Conclusion:

The BEAM is a powerful and versatile virtual machine that has proven its ability to handle demanding workloads. Its focus on concurrency, fault tolerance, and distributed systems makes it an ideal choice for building reliable and scalable applications.

4.2 Processes and Actors in Elixir

Processes in Elixir are lightweight, isolated units of concurrency. They are not operating system processes, but rather virtual processes managed by the Erlang VM (BEAM). This allows Elixir to handle a massive number of concurrent processes efficiently.

Actors are a programming model where concurrent computations are performed by independent actors. In Elixir, each process can be considered an actor. These actors communicate with each other by sending and receiving messages asynchronously.

Key Characteristics of Elixir Processes/Actors:

Isolation: Each process has its own memory space, making them independent and preventing interference between them.

Message Passing: Processes communicate by sending and receiving messages. This asynchronous communication model promotes fault tolerance and scalability.

Lightweight: Processes are lightweight and can be created and destroyed efficiently.

Supervision Trees: Processes can be organized into hierarchical structures called supervision trees. A supervisor process monitors its child processes and can restart them if they fail.

Benefits of Using Processes and Actors:

Scalability: Elixir can handle a large number of concurrent users and requests due to its efficient process model.

Fault Tolerance: If one process fails, it can be restarted without affecting the entire system.

Concurrency: Processes can run concurrently, making it easy to write efficient and responsive applications.

Simplicity: The actor model provides a simple and intuitive way to build concurrent systems.

Example:

```
Elixir
spawn(fn ->
  receive do
    {:ping, pid} ->
      send pid, {:pong}
  end
end)
```

In this example, we spawn a new process that receives a `{:ping, pid}` message. When it receives this message, it sends a `{:pong}` message back to the specified PID.

By understanding and effectively using processes and actors, you can build robust, scalable, and fault-tolerant Elixir applications.

4.3 Message Passing and Supervision Trees

Message Passing

In Elixir, processes communicate with each other asynchronously through message passing. A process sends a message to another process using the `send` function. The receiving process can then process the message using the `receive` construct.

Example:

```
Elixir
# Sender process
send(receiver_pid, {:hello, "world"})
```

```
# Receiver process
receive do
  {:hello, message} ->
    IO.puts "Received: #{message}"
end
```

Key Points:

Asynchronous Communication: Messages are sent without blocking the sender process.

Reliability: Message passing is a reliable mechanism for communication between processes.

Isolation: Processes are isolated, and message passing is the only way for them to interact.

Supervision Trees

A supervision tree is a hierarchical structure of processes, where a supervisor process monitors and restarts its child processes if they fail. This ensures the overall system's reliability and fault tolerance.

Key Components of a Supervision Tree:

Supervisor Process: The root of the tree, responsible for monitoring and restarting its child processes.

Child Processes: Processes that are monitored by a supervisor.

Example:

```
Elixir
Supervisor.start_link(
  [
    {Worker, [arg1, arg2]},
    {AnotherWorker, [arg3]}
```

```
  ],
  strategy: :one_for_one
)
```

In this example, we start a supervisor with two child processes: `Worker` and `AnotherWorker`. The `one_for_one` strategy means that if a child process fails, only that process will be restarted, and the supervisor will continue to monitor the other child processes.

Benefits of Supervision Trees:

Fault Tolerance: By organizing processes into supervision trees, you can ensure that the system recovers from failures.

Scalability: Supervision trees can be easily scaled by adding or removing child processes.

Manageability: Supervision trees provide a structured way to manage and monitor processes.

By effectively using message passing and supervision trees, you can build robust, scalable, and fault-tolerant Elixir applications.

Chapter 5

Concurrency and Parallelism in Elixir

5.1 The Power of the Actor Model

The Actor Model, a cornerstone of Elixir's concurrency paradigm, offers a powerful and elegant approach to building concurrent and distributed systems. It provides a way to structure complex systems into a network of independent actors, each responsible for its own state and behavior.

Key Principles of the Actor Model:

Actors as the Unit of Concurrency: Each actor is a self-contained unit of computation that can receive messages, process them, and send messages to other actors.

Asynchronous Message Passing: Actors communicate with each other by sending and receiving messages asynchronously.[3] This eliminates the need for shared memory and synchronization primitives.

Isolation: Actors are isolated from each other, meaning that they cannot directly access each other's state. This promotes modularity and simplifies reasoning about the system.

Benefits of the Actor Model:

Scalability: The actor model can scale horizontally by adding more actors to the system. This allows for efficient utilization of multiple cores and machines.

Fault Tolerance: Actors can be designed to be fault-tolerant. If an actor fails, it can be restarted without affecting the overall system.

Simplicity: The actor model provides a simple and intuitive way to build concurrent systems.

Flexibility: Actors can be used to model a wide range of systems, from simple to complex.

Elixir's Implementation of the Actor Model:

Elixir leverages the Erlang VM to provide a robust and efficient implementation of the actor model.[9] Each Elixir process is an actor, and the `send` and `receive` constructs are used for message passing.

Example:

```elixir
Elixir
defmodule Counter do
  def start_link do
    spawn(fn ->
      state = 0

      loop do
        receive do
          {:increment} ->
            state = state + 1
            IO.puts "Incremented: #{state}"
          {:decrement} ->
            state = state - 1
            IO.puts "Decremented: #{state}"
        end
        loop
      end
    end)
  end
end
```

In this example, we create a `Counter` actor that maintains an internal state. It can receive `{:increment}` and `{:decrement}` messages, update its state accordingly, and log the new value.

By understanding and effectively using the actor model, you can build complex, scalable, and fault-tolerant Elixir applications.

5.2 Building Concurrent Applications with Elixir

Elixir, built on top of the Erlang VM, is exceptionally well-suited for building concurrent and distributed applications. Its actor model and the underlying BEAM provide a powerful foundation for handling many concurrent tasks efficiently.

Key Concepts for Building Concurrent Applications:

Processes:

Lightweight, isolated units of concurrency.

Communicate via message passing.

Can be easily created and destroyed.

Supervisory Trees:

A hierarchical structure of processes.

A supervisor process monitors and restarts its child processes.

Ensures system reliability and fault tolerance.

Message Passing:

Asynchronous communication between processes.

Prevents race conditions and simplifies concurrency.

Hot Code Swapping:

Update running applications without downtime.

Facilitates continuous deployment and iterative development.

Practical Tips:

Start Small: Begin with simple concurrent tasks and gradually increase complexity.

Leverage the Standard Library: Elixir provides many built-in modules and functions for concurrency, such as Task, Agent, and GenServer.

Use Supervision Trees: Structure your application into a hierarchy of processes to ensure reliability and fault tolerance.

Test Thoroughly: Write comprehensive tests to ensure the correctness of your concurrent code.

Monitor Your Application: Use tools like Observium or Honeycomb to monitor the performance and health of your application.

Example: A Simple Concurrent Counter

```
Elixir
defmodule Counter do
 def start_link do
  spawn(fn ->
   state = 0

   loop do
    receive do
     {:increment} ->
      state = state + 1
```

```
        IO.puts "Incremented: #{state}"
      {:decrement} ->
        state = state - 1
        IO.puts "Decremented: #{state}"
    end
    loop
  end
end)
end
end
```

In this example, we create a simple counter actor that can be incremented or decremented. Multiple processes can send messages to this actor concurrently, and it will handle them efficiently.

Advanced Techniques:

Distributed Systems: Build distributed systems using Elixir's built-in features and libraries like `Erlang/OTP`.

Real-Time Applications: Use Phoenix LiveView for building real-time web applications.

Data Processing Pipelines: Leverage libraries like Broadway for building efficient data processing pipelines.

Machine Learning: Explore libraries like Axon for building machine learning applications.

By mastering these concepts and techniques, you can build highly scalable, fault-tolerant, and efficient Elixir applications.

5.3 Leveraging Parallel Processing in Elixir

Elixir, built on the Erlang VM, is well-suited for parallel processing. Its actor model and the BEAM's efficient process management allow you to harness the power of multiple cores and machines.

Key Techniques for Parallel Processing in Elixir:

1. Task Module:

Simple Parallel Tasks:

Elixir

```
Task.async(fn ->
  # Perform a long-running task
end)
```

Waiting for Results:

Elixir
```
result = Task.await(Task.async(fn ->
  # Perform a task and return a result
end))
```

Parallel Map:

Elixir
```
Enum.map([1, 2, 3], fn x ->
  Task.async(fn -> x * 2 end)
end)
|> Task.await_all
```

2. Agent:

Managing State Concurrently:

Elixir

```elixir
Agent.start(fn -> 0 end)
Agent.update(agent_pid, fn state -> state + 1 end)
```

3. GenServer:

Complex State and Behavior:

Elixir

```elixir
GenServer.start_link(__MODULE__, [])
GenServer.call(pid, {:get_state})
GenServer.cast(pid, {:increment})
```

4. Process Spawning:

Fine-Grained Control:

Elixir

```elixir
spawn(fn ->
  # Perform a task
end)
```

Best Practices for Parallel Processing:

Identify Parallel Tasks: Break down your application into independent tasks that can be executed concurrently.

Avoid Shared Mutable State: Use immutable data structures and message passing to minimize race conditions.

Optimize Task Granularity: Balance the overhead of process creation and message passing with the benefits of parallelism.

Handle Errors Gracefully: Implement proper error handling and recovery mechanisms.

Monitor Performance: Use profiling tools to identify bottlenecks and optimize performance.

Consider Task Distribution: For large-scale applications, explore distributing tasks across multiple machines.

Real-World Use Cases:

Data Processing: Parallel processing can significantly speed up data processing pipelines, such as ETL and data analysis.

Web Applications: Handling concurrent requests and long-running tasks efficiently.

Machine Learning: Training models in parallel can reduce training time.

Game Development: Simulating game worlds and handling player interactions in parallel.

By effectively leveraging Elixir's concurrency primitives and following best practices, you can build highly scalable and performant applications.

Chapter 6

Error Handling and Fault Tolerance

6.1 Error Handling Strategies in Elixir

Elixir, built on the Erlang VM, provides a robust error handling mechanism that helps you build reliable and fault-tolerant applications.

Core Concepts:

Exceptions:

Raised when an error occurs.

Can be caught and handled using `try...catch` expressions.

Useful for unexpected errors.

Process Failures:

Processes can fail due to various reasons, such as exceptions or resource exhaustion.

Supervisor processes monitor child processes and restart them if they fail.

Timeouts:

Can be used to prevent processes from blocking indefinitely.

`receive` expressions can specify timeouts.

Strategies:

Try-Catch Expressions:

Catch and handle exceptions:

Elixir

```
try do
  # Code that might raise an exception
rescue
  e in SomeError ->
    # Handle the specific error
  _error ->
    # Handle other errors
end
```

Process Supervision:
Create a hierarchy of processes.

Supervisor processes monitor and restart child processes.

Configure different restart strategies (one-for-one, one-for-all, rest-for-one).

Timeouts:
Prevent blocking operations:

Elixir

```
receive do
  message ->
    # Handle the message
  after 5000 ->
    # Timeout occurred
```

end

Logging:
Use `Logger` to log errors and warnings.
Configure log levels and formats.

Best Practices:

Early Error Handling: Handle errors as soon as possible to prevent cascading failures.

Informative Error Messages: Provide clear and concise error messages.

Test Error Handling: Write unit tests to ensure that your error handling code works correctly.

Use Supervision Trees: Organize your processes into a hierarchical structure to improve fault tolerance.

Monitor Your Application: Use tools like `Observium` or `Honeycomb` to monitor the health of your application.

Example: A Robust Error Handling Function:

```Elixir
defmodule MyModule do
  def divide(a, b) do
    try do
     a / b
    rescue
     ArithmeticError ->
       IO.puts "Error: Division by zero"
       :error
    end
  end
```

```
end
```

By following these strategies and best practices, you can build robust and resilient Elixir applications that can recover from errors and failures gracefully.

6.2 Supervisor Trees and Process Supervision

A supervisor tree is a hierarchical structure of processes in Elixir, where a supervisor process monitors and restarts its child processes if they fail. This mechanism is crucial for building reliable and fault-tolerant systems.

Key Concepts:

Supervisor Process: The root of the tree, responsible for monitoring and restarting its child processes.

Child Process: A process that is monitored by a supervisor.

Restart Strategy: Determines how a supervisor restarts its child processes when they fail. There are three main strategies:

`one_for_one`: Restarts the failed child process only.

`one_for_all`: Restarts all child processes.

`rest_for_one`: Restarts all child processes except the failed one.

Benefits of Supervision Trees:

Fault Tolerance: By organizing processes into supervision trees, you can ensure that the system recovers from failures.

Scalability: Supervision trees can be easily scaled by adding or removing child processes.

Manageability: Supervision trees provide a structured way to manage and monitor processes.

Example:
Elixir
```elixir
defmodule MySupervisor do
  use Supervisor

  def start_link do
    Supervisor.start_link(__MODULE__, [])
  end

  def init([]) do
    children = [
      worker(MyWorker, [arg1, arg2]),
      worker(AnotherWorker, [arg3])
    ]

    Supervisor.init(children, strategy: :one_for_one)
  end
end
```

In this example:

We define a MySupervisor module that inherits from Supervisor.

The init function specifies the child processes: MyWorker and AnotherWorker.

The `one_for_one` strategy is used, meaning that if a child process fails, only that process will be restarted.

Best Practices:

Clear Supervision Tree Structure: Design a well-structured supervision tree to improve maintainability.

Effective Restart Strategies: Choose the appropriate restart strategy for each child process.

Logging and Monitoring: Use logging to track errors and failures. Monitor the health of your supervision tree.

Testing: Write unit tests to ensure the correctness of your supervisor processes and child processes.

By effectively using supervision trees, you can build robust and reliable Elixir applications that can recover from failures and continue to operate smoothly.

6.3 Building Resilient Applications with Elixir

Elixir, built on the Erlang VM, is renowned for its ability to build highly resilient and fault-tolerant systems. Here are some key strategies to ensure your Elixir applications can withstand failures and continue to operate smoothly:

1. Leverage the Actor Model:

Isolation: Each process is isolated, limiting the impact of failures.

Asynchronous Communication: Message passing ensures that processes can recover from errors and continue processing.

Supervision Trees: Organize processes into a hierarchical structure to monitor and restart failed processes.

2. Implement Robust Error Handling:

Try-Catch Blocks: Handle exceptions gracefully and provide informative error messages.

Process Supervision: Use supervisor processes to monitor and restart failed child processes.

Timeouts: Set timeouts for operations to prevent blocking.

Logging: Log errors and warnings to analyze and troubleshoot issues.

3. Utilize Hot Code Swapping:

Update code in a running application without downtime.

Deploy new features and bug fixes seamlessly.

4. Embrace Distributed Systems:

Distribute your application across multiple nodes to improve scalability and fault tolerance.

Use Elixir's built-in support for distributed systems.

5. Monitor and Alert:

Use tools like `Observium` or `Honeycomb` to monitor your application's performance and health.

Set up alerts to notify you of potential issues.

6. Test Thoroughly:

Write comprehensive unit, integration, and system tests to ensure the reliability of your application.

Use property-based testing to uncover edge cases and unexpected behavior.

7. Consider Redundancy:

Use load balancing to distribute traffic across multiple nodes.

Implement database replication to ensure data availability.

Example: A Resilient Web Application

Elixir

```
defmodule MyWeb.Endpoint do
  use Phoenix.Endpoint

  # ... other configuration

  plug Plug.ErrorHandler
  plug Phoenix.LiveReloader
  plug Plug.Static

  # ... other plugs

  # Plug to handle errors gracefully
  plug MyWeb.Router
end
```

In this example, the `Plug.ErrorHandler` plug is used to handle errors gracefully and provide informative error messages. The `Phoenix.LiveReloader` plug allows for hot code reloading, enabling developers to make changes without restarting the application.

By combining these strategies and leveraging Elixir's powerful features, you can build highly resilient and fault-tolerant applications that can withstand unexpected failures and continue to deliver value to your users.

Chapter 7

Testing and Debugging Elixir Applications

7.1 Unit Testing with ExUnit

ExUnit is Elixir's built-in testing framework, providing a simple and powerful way to write and run tests. It's designed to be easy to learn and use, and it integrates seamlessly with the Elixir ecosystem.

Basic Structure of a Test Case

A test case in ExUnit is a module that inherits from `ExUnit.Case`. Each test case contains one or more test functions, which are defined using the `test` macro.

```elixir
Elixir
defmodule MyModuleTest do
  use ExUnit.Case
  import MyModule

  test "calculates factorial of 5" do
    assert factorial(5) == 120
  end
end
```

Key Features of ExUnit:

Assert Macros: ExUnit provides a variety of assert macros to check the correctness of your code:

`assert`: Asserts that a given expression is true.

`refute`: Asserts that a given expression is false.

`assert_equal`: Asserts that two values are equal.

`assert_not_equal`: Asserts that two values are not equal.

`assert_match`: Asserts that a value matches a given pattern.

And many more...

Test Fixtures: You can define test fixtures to set up and tear down test environments.

Test Hooks: You can define `setup` and `teardown` hooks to run code before and after each test.

Test Organization: Organize tests into test modules and test cases for better structure.

Test Output: ExUnit provides clear and concise test output, including test results, error messages, and code coverage reports.

Running Tests:

To run tests, use the `mix test` command in your terminal. ExUnit will automatically discover and run all tests in your project.

Best Practices for Unit Testing:

Test Every Function: Write test cases for all public functions in your modules.

Isolate Tests: Each test should be independent and not rely on the state of other tests.

Use Test Fixtures: Set up and tear down test environments to ensure consistent test results.

Write Clear and Concise Tests: Use descriptive test names and assertions.

Cover Edge Cases: Test for both normal and edge-case inputs.

Use Property-Based Testing: Consider using tools like PropEr to generate random test cases and increase test coverage.

By following these best practices and leveraging ExUnit's powerful features, you can write high-quality, reliable Elixir code.

7.2 Property-Based Testing with PropEr

Property-based testing is a powerful technique that complements traditional unit testing. Instead of writing specific test cases, you define properties that your code should satisfy, and PropEr generates random inputs to test these properties. This approach can uncover unexpected edge cases and improve code quality.

How PropEr Works:

Define Properties: You write properties as functions that take random inputs and assert that the output satisfies certain conditions.

Generate Inputs: PropEr generates random inputs based on the property's signature.

Test Execution: PropEr runs the property with the generated inputs and checks if the assertion holds.

Shrinking: If a test fails, PropEr attempts to find a simpler input that still causes the failure. This helps in debugging and understanding the root cause of the issue.

Example:

```elixir
Elixir
defmodule MyModuleTest do
  use ExUnit.Case
  import PropEr

  test "list_length" do
    property do
      list <- list_of(integer())
      assert length(list) == Enum.count(list)
    end
  end
end
```

In this example, we define a property that asserts that the `length` function returns the same result as the `Enum.count` function for any given list. PropEr will generate various random lists to test this property.

Benefits of Property-Based Testing:

Increased Test Coverage: PropEr can uncover edge cases that might be missed by traditional unit testing.

Improved Code Quality: By finding and fixing bugs early, property-based testing can lead to more reliable and robust code.

Reduced Test Maintenance: Property-based tests can be more concise and easier to maintain than traditional unit tests.

Best Practices for Property-Based Testing:

Start Small: Begin with simple properties and gradually increase complexity.

Use Clear and Concise Properties: Define properties that are easy to understand and reason about.

Choose Appropriate Generators: Use generators that produce realistic and relevant inputs.

Consider Performance: Be mindful of the performance implications of property-based testing, especially for large-scale tests.

Combine with Traditional Unit Testing: Use property-based testing to complement traditional unit testing.

By incorporating property-based testing into your development workflow, you can significantly improve the quality and reliability of your Elixir applications.

7.3 Debugging Techniques in Elixir

Elixir provides a variety of tools and techniques to help you debug your applications effectively. Here are some of the most common ones:

1. IEx Shell:

Interactive Debugging: Use the `iex` shell to inspect variables, evaluate expressions, and step through code.

Remote Debugging: Connect to a running application and debug it remotely.

2. Logger:

Logging Messages: Use the `Logger` module to log messages to the console or a file.

Customizing Logs: Configure log levels, formats, and backends.

3. Debugger:

Step-by-Step Execution: Use the debugger to step through code line by line.

Inspect Variables: Examine the values of variables at any point during execution.

Set Breakpoints: Pause execution at specific points in the code.

4. Process Observer:

Monitor Process Behavior: Use `:observer` to monitor the state of processes and their messages.

Identify Performance Bottlenecks: Analyze process metrics like CPU usage and memory consumption.

5. Error Handling and Logging:

Handle Exceptions: Use `try...catch` blocks to catch and handle exceptions gracefully.

Log Errors: Log detailed error messages to help with debugging.

Tips for Effective Debugging:

Break Down Complex Problems: Divide complex problems into smaller, more manageable parts.

Use `IO.inspect` for Quick Debugging: Temporarily print values to the console to inspect them.

Leverage the `iex` Shell: Use the `iex` shell to experiment with code and test hypotheses.

Write Clear and Concise Code: Well-structured code is easier to debug.

Use a Good Code Editor: A good code editor with features like syntax highlighting, code completion, and debugging tools can significantly improve your debugging experience.

By combining these techniques and following best practices, you can effectively debug your Elixir applications and identify and fix issues quickly.

Chapter 8

Deploying Elixir Applications

8.1 Deployment Strategies for Elixir Applications

Elixir offers various deployment strategies to deploy your applications efficiently and reliably. Here are some common approaches:

1. Mix Releases:

Self-contained Deployments: Creates standalone releases that can be deployed to any environment.

Configuration Management: Easily manage configuration settings for different environments.

Hot Code Swapping: Deploy updates without downtime.

2. Docker:

Containerization: Packages your application and its dependencies into a container.

Portability: Deploy to any environment that supports Docker.

Scalability: Easily scale your application by deploying multiple containers.

3. Kubernetes:

Container Orchestration: Manages and scales containerized applications.

High Availability: Ensures continuous availability through automatic failover and load balancing.

Scalability: Automatically scales your application based on demand.

4. Heroku:

Platform as a Service (PaaS): Provides a platform for deploying and managing applications.

Easy Deployment: Deploy your application with a single command.

Automatic Scaling: Scales your application based on traffic.

5. AWS, GCP, or Azure:

Infrastructure as a Service (IaaS): Provides infrastructure resources like virtual machines, storage, and networking.

Custom Deployments: Tailor your deployment to specific needs.

Scalability: Scale your application by adding or removing instances.

Best Practices for Deployment:

Automated Deployments: Use tools like `mix release` or CI/CD pipelines to automate deployments.

Configuration Management: Use configuration management tools like `Config` to manage environment-specific settings.

Monitoring and Logging: Monitor your application's performance and health using tools like `Honeycomb` or `Prometheus`.

Testing: Thoroughly test your application in different environments to ensure smooth deployments.

Rollback Strategy: Have a plan for rolling back to a previous version if a deployment fails.

By following these strategies and best practices, you can deploy your Elixir applications efficiently and reliably.

8.2 Using Deployment Tools: Distillery and Mix Releases

Elixir provides powerful tools to streamline the deployment process. Two of the most popular options are Distillery and Mix Releases.

Distillery

Distillery is a tool for packaging and deploying Elixir applications. It creates self-contained releases, making it easier to deploy your application to various environments.

Key Features:

Self-contained Releases: Packages your application and its dependencies into a single directory.

Configuration Management: Allows you to manage configuration settings for different environments.

Hot Code Swapping: Supports hot code swapping for seamless updates.

Basic Usage:

Bash
mix release

This command will create a release directory containing the compiled application and its dependencies. You can then deploy this release to any environment that supports the Erlang VM.

Mix Releases

Mix Releases is a built-in feature of the `mix` tool that provides a simpler way to create releases. It's suitable for smaller applications and simpler deployment scenarios.

Basic Usage:

Bash
mix release

This command will create a release directory, similar to Distillery.

Choosing Between Distillery and Mix Releases:

Distillery: For complex applications with specific deployment needs, Distillery offers more flexibility and control.

Mix Releases: For simpler applications, Mix Releases provides a straightforward approach to creating releases.

Best Practices for Deployment:

Configuration Management: Use configuration files to manage environment-specific settings.

Logging and Monitoring: Implement robust logging and monitoring to track application performance and identify issues.

Error Handling: Handle errors gracefully and provide informative error messages.

Security: Secure your deployments by following security best practices, such as using strong passwords and limiting access to sensitive information.

Testing: Thoroughly test your application before deploying it to production.

By leveraging these tools and following best practices, you can deploy your Elixir applications efficiently and reliably.

8.3 Monitoring and Logging Elixir Applications

Effective monitoring and logging are crucial for maintaining the health and performance of your Elixir applications.[1]Here are some key strategies and tools:

Logging:

Logger Module: Elixir's built-in Logger module provides a flexible and powerful way to log messages to the console or a file.

Log Levels: Configure log levels (debug, info, warn, error, fatal) to control the verbosity of your logs.

Custom Log Formats: Customize the format of log messages to include timestamps, process IDs, and other relevant information.

Log Backends: Use different backends (e.g., file, database, or remote logging services) to store and analyze logs.

Monitoring:

Process Observer: The :observer tool provides a visual interface to monitor the state of processes, messages, and system metrics.

Metrics Libraries: Use libraries like `Metrics` or `Telemetrics` to collect and expose metrics.

Remote Monitoring: Use tools like `Honeycomb` or `Datadog` to monitor your application's performance and health remotely.

Alerting: Set up alerts to notify you of potential issues, such as high CPU usage, slow response times, or errors.

Best Practices:

Log Meaningful Information: Include relevant details like timestamps, process IDs, and error messages.

Rotate Log Files: Regularly rotate log files to prevent them from growing too large.

Use Structured Logging: Log structured data (e.g., JSON) for easier analysis.

Monitor Key Metrics: Track metrics like response time, error rates, and resource usage.

Correlate Logs and Metrics: Use correlation IDs to link related log entries and metrics.

Automate Monitoring: Set up automated monitoring and alerting to proactively identify and resolve issues.

Tools and Techniques:

Elixir's Built-in Tools: `Logger` and `:observer`

Third-Party Libraries: `Metrics`, `Telemetrics`

Cloud-Based Monitoring: Honeycomb, Datadog, New Relic

Logging Backends: File, database, or remote logging services

Alerting Systems: PagerDuty, Opsgenie

By effectively monitoring and logging your Elixir applications, you can quickly identify and resolve issues, improve performance, and ensure the overall health of your system.

Chapter 9

Advanced Elixir Topics

9.1 Metaprogramming with Macros in Elixir

Metaprogramming is a powerful technique that allows you to manipulate the syntax and structure of your language at compile time. In Elixir, macros provide a flexible and expressive way to extend the language itself.

Understanding Macros

Syntax Expansion: Macros expand into Elixir code before compilation.

Hygiene: Macros ensure that variables and functions defined within them don't conflict with variables and functions in the surrounding code.

Quote and Unquote: The `quote` and `unquote` operators are used to manipulate syntax trees.

Creating a Simple Macro

Elixir
```
defmodule MyMacros do
  defmacro greet(name) do
    quote do
      IO.puts "Hello, #{unquote(name)}!"
    end
  end
end
```

Usage:

Elixir
import MyMacros

greet("Alice")

This will output:

Hello, Alice!

Common Use Cases for Macros

Domain-Specific Languages (DSLs): Create custom syntax for specific domains.

Code Generation: Automatically generate code based on patterns.

Metaprogramming: Manipulate the syntax tree to create new language constructs.

Testing: Generate test cases dynamically.

Advanced Macro Techniques

Quote and Unquote: Control the expansion of code.

Hygiene: Ensure that macros don't introduce naming conflicts.

Recursive Macros: Define macros that call themselves recursively.

Macro-Generated Code: Generate complex code structures at compile time.

Cautions and Best Practices

Complexity: Macros can make code harder to understand and maintain. Use them judiciously.

Testing: Thoroughly test code that uses macros to ensure correctness.

Readability: Write clear and concise macros.

Performance: Be aware of the performance implications of complex macros.

By mastering macros, you can create elegant, concise, and powerful Elixir code. However, remember to use them responsibly and consider the trade-offs between expressiveness and maintainability.

9.2 OTP Behaviors and GenServers

The Open Telecom Platform (OTP) is a framework for building distributed, fault-tolerant systems. It is a core component of the Erlang VM and is available to Elixir developers through the `GenServer` behavior.

GenServers

A GenServer is a generic server process that follows a specific protocol for handling requests and updates. It's a fundamental building block for building concurrent and fault-tolerant systems in Elixir.

Key Components of a GenServer:

State: Stores the current state of the GenServer.

Initialization: The `init/1` function initializes the GenServer's state.

Handling Calls: The `handle_call/3` function handles synchronous requests.

Handling Casts: The `handle_cast/2` function handles asynchronous messages.

Updating State: The `handle_info/2` function handles asynchronous messages that can update the state.

Termination: The `terminate/2` function is called when the GenServer is terminated.

Example:

```elixir
Elixir
defmodule CounterServer do
  use GenServer

  def start_link(initial_value \\ 0) do
    GenServer.start_link(__MODULE__, initial_value)
  end

  def init(initial_value) do
    {:ok, initial_value}
  end

  def handle_call(:get_value, _from, state) do
    {:reply, state, state}
  end
```

```
def handle_cast(:increment, state) do
  {:noreply, state + 1}
end
end
```

Other OTP Behaviors

Supervisor: Manages and restarts child processes.

Worker: A simple process that performs tasks.

Generic Server: A more flexible version of GenServer.

Finite State Machine: Models finite state machines.

Agent: A simple process for storing and updating state.

By understanding and effectively using OTP behaviors, you can build robust, scalable, and fault-tolerant Elixir applications.

9.3 Real-Time Applications with Phoenix Framework

Phoenix is a powerful and productive web framework built on top of Elixir.[1] It's particularly well-suited for building real-time applications, thanks to its seamless integration with the Erlang VM's concurrency and fault-tolerance features.

Core Concepts

Channels: Phoenix Channels provide a robust and scalable way to build real-time features like chat, notifications, and collaborative editing.

PubSub: A publish-subscribe pattern for broadcasting messages to multiple clients.

WebSockets: A protocol for bidirectional communication between the client and server.

Building a Real-Time Chat Application

Here's a basic outline of how to build a real-time chat application using Phoenix:

Create a Phoenix Project:

Bash

mix phx.new chat_app

Define the Channel: Create a ChatChannel module to handle real-time communication:

Elixir

```
defmodule ChatAppWeb.ChatChannel do
  use Phoenix.Channel

  def join("room:" <> room_id, _message, socket) do
    {:ok, socket}
  end

  def handle_in("new_msg", %{"message" => message}, socket) do
    broadcast socket, "new_msg", %{user: socket.assigns.user_id, message: message}
    {:noreply, socket}
  end
end
```

Create the Frontend: Use a frontend framework like React, Vue, or a Phoenix LiveView to build the user interface. The frontend will connect to the Phoenix backend using WebSockets and send/receive messages.

Deploy: Deploy your application to a platform like Heroku, AWS, or GCP.

Key Benefits of Phoenix for Real-Time Applications

Scalability: The Erlang VM can handle a large number of concurrent connections efficiently.

Fault Tolerance: Phoenix applications are highly resilient to failures.

Real-Time Features: Channels provide a powerful way to build real-time features.

Productivity: The Phoenix framework is designed to be productive and efficient.

By leveraging Phoenix's powerful features, you can build scalable and reliable real-time applications.

Phoenix LiveView: A powerful framework for building interactive web interfaces without full page reloads.

Optimizing Performance: Strategies for optimizing the performance of real-time applications.

Security: Best practices for securing real-time applications.

Testing Real-Time Applications: Effective testing strategies for real-time features.

Chapter 10

The Future of Elixir

10.1 Emerging Trends and Technologies in Elixir

Elixir, a functional programming language built on the Erlang VM, continues to evolve and adapt to the ever-changing technological landscape. Here are some of the most promising emerging trends and technologies in the Elixir ecosystem:

1. Phoenix LiveView

Server-Rendered, Real-Time User Interfaces: Phoenix LiveView allows you to build rich, interactive user interfaces without relying heavily on JavaScript.

Reduced Client-Side Complexity: Less JavaScript means fewer potential bugs and performance issues.

Hot Reloading: Changes to your code are instantly reflected in the browser.

2. Data Science and Machine Learning:

Nx: A numerical computing library for Elixir, enabling you to perform numerical computations, linear algebra, and machine learning tasks.

Integration with Python: Leverage Python's extensive data science ecosystem through libraries like `ex_py` and `NIFs`.

3. Distributed Systems:

Elixir's Strong Suit: The Erlang VM's built-in support for distributed systems makes Elixir ideal for building scalable and fault-tolerant applications.

Distributed Erlang: Explore advanced techniques for distributing Elixir applications across multiple nodes.

4. Functional Programming Paradigms:

Advanced Functional Techniques: Deepen your understanding of functional programming concepts like higher-order functions, recursion, and algebraic data types.

Property-Based Testing: Use tools like PropEr to write more robust and comprehensive tests.

5. WebAssembly:

Running Elixir Code in the Browser: Explore the potential of WebAssembly to run Elixir code directly in the browser.

Hybrid Applications: Combine the power of Elixir's backend with WebAssembly's frontend capabilities.

6. Serverless Computing:

Elixir and Serverless: Explore how Elixir can be used to build serverless functions and microservices.

Leverage Cloud Providers: Utilize serverless platforms like AWS Lambda or Google Cloud Functions to deploy Elixir functions.

7. Quantum Computing:

Quantum Elixir: While still in its early stages, explore the potential of Elixir for quantum computing and quantum algorithms.

By staying up-to-date with these trends, you can leverage the power of Elixir to build innovative and cutting-edge applications.

10.2 The Thriving Elixir Community and Ecosystem

The Elixir community is vibrant and rapidly growing. It's characterized by its friendly and supportive nature, as well as its dedication to building high-quality software.

Key Aspects of the Elixir Community:

Active Forums and Communities: Platforms like the Elixir Forum and the Elixir subreddit provide a space for developers to ask questions, share knowledge, and collaborate.

Regular Conferences and Meetups: Numerous conferences, such as ElixirConf, ElixirConf EU, and local meetups, bring together Elixir enthusiasts from around the world.

Open-Source Libraries and Frameworks: A rich ecosystem of open-source libraries and frameworks, including Phoenix, Ecto, and Nerves, is available to accelerate development.

Strong Corporate Backing: Companies like WhatsApp and Discord have adopted Elixir for their production systems, demonstrating its reliability and scalability.

Future of the Elixir Ecosystem:

The future of Elixir looks promising. With its strong foundation, active community, and focus on productivity and scalability, Elixir is well-positioned to continue growing in popularity.

Here are some potential areas of growth:

Increased Adoption: As more companies recognize the benefits of Elixir, we can expect to see wider adoption in various industries.

Maturity of the Ecosystem: The Elixir ecosystem will continue to mature, with new libraries and frameworks emerging to address a broader range of use cases.

Integration with Other Technologies: Elixir can be integrated with other technologies, such as JavaScript and Python, to create powerful hybrid applications.

Innovation and Experimentation: The community will continue to experiment with new ideas and technologies, pushing the boundaries of what's possible with Elixir.

By staying engaged with the community, contributing to open-source projects, and keeping up with the latest trends, you can be part of the exciting future of Elixir.

10.3 Elixir's Role in the Future of Programming

Elixir, with its functional programming paradigm, strong concurrency model, and fault-tolerance features, is poised to play a significant role in the future of programming.[1] Here are some key areas where Elixir is making a difference:

1. Real-Time Applications

Phoenix Framework: Elixir's Phoenix framework is a powerful tool for building real-time web applications, such as chat apps, collaborative tools, and online gaming platforms.

Scalability and Performance: Elixir's ability to handle high concurrency and low latency makes it ideal for real-time applications.

2. Distributed Systems

Fault Tolerance: Elixir's built-in fault-tolerance mechanisms make it suitable for building distributed systems that can recover from failures.

Scalability: Elixir's actor model allows for easy scaling of applications across multiple nodes.

Distributed Erlang: Leverage the power of the Erlang VM for building large-scale distributed systems.

3. Data Processing Pipelines

Parallel Processing: Elixir's concurrency features enable efficient parallel processing of large datasets.

Fault Tolerance: Ensure data integrity and reliability in data pipelines.

Scalability: Handle increasing data volumes and complex processing tasks.

4. IoT and Embedded Systems

Nerves Framework: Build embedded devices and IoT applications with Elixir.

Low-Latency and High-Reliability: Elixir's strong foundation in real-time systems makes it suitable for IoT applications.

5. Functional Programming Paradigm

Clean and Concise Code: Elixir's functional approach promotes writing clear and maintainable code.

Immutability: Reduces side effects and makes code easier to reason about.

Parallelism and Concurrency: The functional paradigm is well-suited for concurrent and parallel programming.

While Elixir may not be as widely adopted as languages like Python or JavaScript, its unique strengths make it a valuable tool for developers who are looking to build reliable, scalable, and maintainable applications. As the demand for high-performance, fault-tolerant systems continues to grow, Elixir is well-positioned to become an increasingly important language in the future of programming.

www.ingramcontent.com/pod-product-compliance
Lightning Source LLC
LaVergne TN
LVHW051740050326
832903LV00023B/1027